D1709423

Z**oo**m In on
Great Women

Anne Frank

Jennifer Strand

abdopublishing.com

Published by Abdo Zoom™, PO Box 398166, Minneapolis, Minnesota 55439. Copyright © 2017 by Abdo Consulting Group, Inc. International copyrights reserved in all countries. No part of this book may be reproduced in any form without written permission from the publisher. Abdo Zoom™ is a trademark and logo of Abdo Consulting Group, Inc.

Printed in the United States of America, North Mankato, Minnesota
072016
092016

THIS BOOK CONTAINS RECYCLED MATERIALS

Cover Photo: DPA/Corbis
Interior Photos: DPA/Corbis, 1; Anne Frank Fonds Basel/Getty Images, 4, 7; Leo La Valle/EPA/Newscom, 5; iStockphoto, 6–7; Charles Russell Collection/National Archives and Records Administration, 9; akg-images/Newscom, 10, 18–19; Public Domain, 11; akg-images/Michael Teller/Newscom, 12; World History Archive/Newscom, 14; Evert Elzinga/AP Images, 15; Massimo Catarinella/iStockphoto, 16; Ronald W. Jansen/iStockphoto, 17

Editor: Brienna Rossiter
Series Designer: Madeline Berger
Art Direction: Dorothy Toth

Publisher's Cataloging-in-Publication Data
Names: Strand, Jennifer, author.
Title: Anne Frank / by Jennifer Strand.
Description: Minneapolis, MN : Abdo Zoom, [2017] | Series: Great women |
    Includes bibliographical references and index.
Identifiers: LCCN 2016941356 | ISBN 9781680792201 (lib. bdg.) |
    ISBN 9781680793888 (ebook) | 9781680794779 (Read-to-me ebook)
Subjects: LCSH: Frank, Anne, 1929-1945--Juvenile literature. | Jews--
    Netherlands--Amsterdam--Biography--Juvenile literature. | Holocaust, Jewish
    (1939-1945)--Netherlands--Amsterdam--Biography--Juvenile literature. |
    World War, 1939-1945--Jews--Juvenile literature. | Amsterdam (Netherlands)
    --Biography--Juvenile literature.
Classification: DDC 940.53 [B]--dc23
LC record available at http://lccn.loc.gov/2016941356

Table of Contents

Introduction

Anne Frank lived during
World War II (1939–1945).

4

Her family faced many **hardships**.
She wrote about them in a diary.
It was made into a book.

Early Life

Anne was born on June 12, 1929.

Her family was Jewish.
They lived in Germany.

Life there was hard.
Many people were poor.
The **Nazis** blamed Jewish people.

They discriminated against them.

Leader

Anne's family moved
to the Netherlands.

The Nazis took control there, too. They sent groups of people to **labor camps**. Jewish people were in danger.

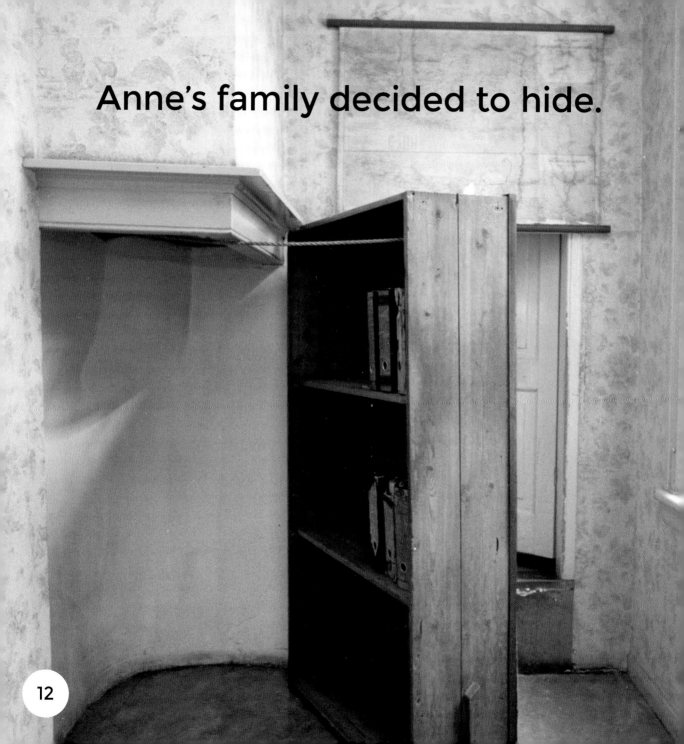

Anne's family decided to hide.

They moved to a secret **annex**. They had to stay quiet. Sometimes they did not have much food.

Anne kept a diary.

14

She wrote about her life. She wrote about her thoughts and feelings.

Anne's family hid for two years. Then Nazis found the annex. They sent Anne's family to labor camps.

Many people there were killed.
Anne died in 1945. She was only 15.

The war ended soon after. Anne's father found her diary.

He helped **publish** it.
Many people read it.
The diary helped them
learn about this time.

Anne Frank

Born: June 12, 1929

Birthplace: Frankfurt, Germany

Known For: Anne wrote *Anne Frank: The Diary of a Young Girl*. It helped people learn about the time known as the Holocaust.

Died: February 1945

Key Dates

1929: Annelies Marie Frank is born on June 12.

1933: Anne's family moves to the Netherlands to escape the Nazis.

1942: Anne's family starts hiding in a secret annex.

1944: Nazis send Anne and her family to a labor camp called Auschwitz.

1945: Anne dies in a labor camp.

1947: Anne's father helps publish her diary.

Glossary

annex - a building that is attached to a larger building.

discriminated - treated a group of people unfairly.

hardships - things that cause pain.

labor camp - a place where people are forced to do hard work.

Nazis - a group that controlled Germany from 1933 to 1945.

publish – to create a book so that others can read it.

Booklinks

For more information
on **Anne Frank**, please visit
booklinks.abdopublishing.com

Z♀m In on Biographies!

Learn even more with the Abdo Zoom
Biographies database. Check out
abdozoom.com for more information.

Index